Row, row, row your boat
Gently down the stream.
Merrily, merrily, merrily, merrily,
Life is but a dream.
—Traditional English folk song

Happiness is the endless realization of an infinite dream.
—George Ohsawa

Dream Diagnosis

What Dreams Reveal About
Your Health, Relationships,
Fortune, and Destiny

By Michio Kushi
with Edward Esko
Foreword by Alex Jack

One Peaceful World Press
Becket, Massachusetts

Dream Diagnosis

For further information on mail-order sales, wholesale or retail discounts, distribution, translations, and foreign rights, please contact the publisher:

One Peaceful World Press
P.O. Box 10
Leland Road
Becket, MA 01223
U.S.A.

Telephone (413) 623-2322
Fax (413) 623-8827

First Edition: February 1996
10 9 8 7 6 5 4 3 2 1

ISBN 1–882984–18-8
Printed in U.S.A.

Contents

Foreword

"An uninterpreted dream is like an unopened letter."
—Zohar

Dreams have intrigued, challenged, and puzzled human beings since the earliest times. In ancient civilizations, kings relied on prophets such as Joseph and Daniel who could understand the language of dreams. In the modern era, Descartes, Kellogg, and other scientists and inventors have attributed their insights and discoveries to dreams.

In recent times, theories and schools of dream interpretation have multiplied. Freud saw dreams primarily as symbols of repressed sexual desires, while Jung viewed them as archetypes of the collective unconscious.

In our holistic era, the limitations of such views have become obvious. Human beings cannot be reduced to only one dimension. Where Freud fixated on the first chakra to explain human behavior, Jung focused narrowly on the top chakra.

In between, there are five other chakras and the merdians, organs, and functions of the mind/body, as well as the infinite universe and its eternal order of which we are a small part.

In *Dream Diagnosis,* Michio Kushi offers a comprehensive approach to understanding dreams. He supplies the missing chakras, especially that governing matters of the heart, but also the everyday world of life, work, study, travel, nature, animals, health, and happiness. He offers endless insight into the nature and quality of dreams based on his own dream journal, kept over many years, as well as the traditional wisdom and understanding of the Far East.

Food, as he explains, is the foundation of life, and often our dreams reflect the condition of our inner organs and vital functions. Over the years, I have learned to diagnose my own day to day health using some of the dream symbols introduced in this book and very practically made adjustments the next day to compensate for too much salt, sweets, or liquid conumed the day before.

But beyond our nightly dreams and what they have to teach us, Michio explains the relation of dreaming to daydreams, surface consciousness, and the subconscious. He inspires us to create our own image and life dream and bring that into reality.

While each of us must discover our own dream in life, we all share a common dream of a world of enduring health and peace in which our originality can be expressed. By eating together in a spirit of gratitude and appreciating nature around us, we develop a similar mind and spirit and are able to contribute to the realization of one peaceful world.

Alex Jack
October 24, 1995
Becket, Massachusetts

1
Interpreting Dreams

The interpretation of dreams is nothing more than another application of yin and yang. In the Orient, there are several interesting proverbs concerning dreams:

> A sage does not dream.
> The foolish man tries to interpret dreams.
> Dreams evidence illness in the organs.

For thousands of years these proverbs were the traditional way of looking at dreams. The sage does not dream, because most dreams are imaginary, they are not a part of wisdom. But there is an exception: among many dreams, there are some which are true dreams. They do not often occur, but they are there occasionally. So the sage does not experience the many imaginary dreams, but what he may have is an occasional true dream. A macrobiotic person will also have this kind of dream, not the usual one which so many people have.

If you do have many dreams, then this is a sign that you have disorders in your internal organs. Chaos is there, your brain is in disorder. That is why you are seeing dreams. When you are having a nightmare, you are not having a true dream. You are experiencing the disorder of your internal organs. It is an illusion.

A true dream appears when you are in deep sleep. Illusory dreams happen when you are half awake. The first two to three hours of sleep are the deepest. After that your sleep becomes shallow. At that time you will see various illusory dreams. A true dream comes during the deepest sleep. If you take stimulants like coffee or hot spices, these interfere with deep sleep, and as a result, you will not be able to have a true dream. You will have only illusory dreams.

A healthy person can sleep for three to five hours a night, have deep and refreshing sleep, as well as true dreams. And if you are really healthy, you can shorten your sleeping time to three hours each night, especially after you are sixty years old. A healthy person requires only three hours of sleep a night. However, when you are not healthy and you sleep for a long time, that is when you have illusory dreams.

Now, the second saying: "The foolish man tries to interpret dreams." Many people have tried to interpret dreams. Freud is an example of a man who is thought to be wise, but who was an interpreter of dreams. Thinking such as this is foolish. The reason it is foolish is because ninety-nine percent of all dreams are illusory. Only one percent of dreams are true dreams.

When we use dreams for judging or determining the future, we must only use the true dreams. We must not use the fragmented, illusory dreams. This latter type of dream only evidences your sickness or imbalance. It can be used only to diagnose the condition of your internal organs. But for proper judgment of the future, we must use only the true dream.

An example of a true dream, and the correct interpretation of it, can be found in the Bible, in the Book of Genesis, in the story of Joseph:

> And Pharaoh said unto Joseph, In my dream, behold, I stood upon the bank of the river: And, behold, there came up out of the river seven kine, fatfleshed and well favoured; and they fed in a meadow. And behold, seven other kine came up after them, poor and very ill favoured and leanfleshed, such as I never saw in all the land of Egypt for badness: And the lean and the ill favoured kine did eat up the first seven fat kine: And when they had eaten them up, it could not be known

that they had eaten them; but they were still ill favoured, as at the beginning. So I awoke.

And I saw in my dream, and, behold, seven ears came up in one stalk, full and good: And behold, seven ears, withered, thin, and blasted with the east wind, sprung up after them; And the thin ears devoured the seven good ears: and I told this unto the magicians; but there was none that could declare it to me.

And Joseph said unto Pharaoh, The dream of Pharaoh is one: God hath shewed Pharaoh what he is about to do. The seven good kine are seven years; and the seven good ears are seven years: the dream is one. And the seven thin and ill favoured kine that came up after them are seven years; and the seven empty ears blasted with the east wind shall be seven years of famine.

Behold, there come seven years of great plenty throughout all the land of Egypt: And there shall arise after them seven years of famine; and all the plenty shall be forgotten in the land of Egypt; and the famine shall consume the land; And the plenty shall not be known in the land by reason of that famine following; for it shall be very grievous. And for that the dream was doubled unto Pharaoh twice; it is because the thing is established by God, and God will shortly bring it to pass.

When the Pharaoh saw the dream of seven fat calves being eaten by the seven lean calves, and seven full ears of grain being devoured by seven withered ears, this was a true dream. It held a real meaning for the future of Egypt. Joseph interpreted it to mean that Egypt would have seven years of plentiful harvest, followed by seven years of famine. Because of the correct interpretation of this dream, Joseph was able to guide the Pharaoh to store excess grain from the plentiful years for use during the seven years of famine. In this way the people of Egypt were spared the hardship of hunger and starvation.

Simply put, the difference between a true dream and a non-true, illusory dream is that in a true dream, you can remember it from beginning to end. You remember the dream clearly, and can easily recall it. But a non-true dream is somewhat obscure. It will demand extra effort for you to reconstruct the whole sequence of the dream. And you can never be quite certain whether the dream really did go this way or that way. Or you may forget part of it here and there.

True dreams can be divided into four large categories:

1. **Dreams of Heaven** These include dreams in which you see the sky, clouds, stars, sun, moon, thunder, rain, snow, frost, mist, a rainbow, celestial bodies, or weather.

2. **Dreams of Earth** These include dreams in which you see the sea, trees, flowers, the earth, forests, rivers, rocks, mountains, streams, animals, and water.

3. **Dreams of Humanity** These include dreams of people, such as relatives, friends, angels, ghosts, children, juniors or seniors, society, your company, business, town, or city, or events such as parties, celebrations, or funerals.

4. **Miscellaneous Dreams** These include a combination of the above.

These true dreams often appear in symbolic form, and therefore require interpretation. Sometimes events appear clearly, and these events will happen later exactly as the appeared in the dream. But usually these dreams appear in the form of symbols.

One well known person who had such prophetic dreams was Abraham Lincoln. Soon after winning the presidential election in 1860, Lincoln was resting half asleep on a lounge in his study. He saw a double image of himself in a mirror. One image was normal, the other, pale and ghostly. Lincoln believed that the lifelike image signified he would live through his first term as president, while the ghostlike image meant he would die before completing his second term.

Several weeks before his assassination, Lincoln saw a dream of his own funeral.

The events that followed Lincoln's dream happened in a way that was similar to the actual dream. But usually true dreams appear in symbolic form. If the symbols are expressed in terms of numbers of things—like seven oxen—then this can be interpreted as numbers of days, years, people, or other things. The number of things seen in the dream can refer to repeated events or the number of days or years the events will happen.

As an example, suppose a businessman dreams he is swimming in the ocean. A big wave appears and crashes over him and he disappears. Then he comes to the surface. Then another wave appears and again crashes over him. Again he disappears under the water and finally resurfaces. This is repeated four times. After all these struggles he manages to find dry land or a big rock, and he emerges from the water. This dream can be interpreted to mean that he will experience many troubles in the business world. His business may become almost bankrupt. There may be periods of recovery, but then the difficulty will return. This will be repeated four times before he will reach a final period of stabilization. Only then will his business become prosperous.

Seeing a True Dream

In order to see a true dream, two conditions must exist: 1) your whole body, including the brain, is healthy and pure; and 2) your attention is focused on the problem you are trying to solve or the condition about which you are concerned.

If you are involved in something and do not know whether it will be successful or not, and you would like to know its outcome, you can make a true dream happen. Before you go to sleep, relax and breathe deeply. Be as calm as possible. Breathe in three times, then breathe out in one long breath. When you are breathing in, hold the breath you had before so that you are continually adding more breath to the breath already taken in. Then breathe out in one long stream of breath. While you are doing this, bring into your mind what you would like to achieve, what you would like to know.

Then you can lie down in your bed all the time keeping in mind the image of what you would like to know. Then fall asleep. In this way you can cause a true dream to occur. If you are eating well the quality of this dream will be good. But if you are eating ice cream or hamburgers, then you will, more than likely, have only a fragmented, illusory dream.

Please try this method for yourself. If you are, however, not serious, then the dream will not be serious. It must be a really serious matter.

Seeing Your Loved-One in a Dream

There is another kind of dream you can cause to happen. Probably many of you would like to see an image of your sweetheart in your dreams. This you can easily do. Again, you have to be serious, otherwise the vision will not appear. You must really be seeking him or her, and you must really want to see his or her image.

Before you go to sleep, lie on your bed and relax completely. Be as quiet as possible. Then breathe into the heart region of your chest; breathe deeply in and out. At the same time form a mental image of your sweetheart. While doing this you may place your hand over your heart. After you have breathed deeply in your heart region for five or ten times, hold your left hand up. With your right index finger write the name of your sweetheart on the palm of your left hand. Do this three times. Then take the name you have written on the left palm and drink it. Place your hand over your mouth as if you are going to drink the name. Do this three times. Do this slowly and deliberately. Then go to sleep. The vision of your sweetheart will come. Very interesting, isn't it? This is a traditional method for visualizing your sweetheart in your dreams—especially when that person is far away.

Waking Up Without a Clock

Are you able to get up at exactly the time you wish to, without the use of an alarm clock? A truly healthy person is able to do this all the time. There is a practice you can use to develop this ability. Again, lie on your bed and relax. Before you fall asleep repeat five or ten times, “I will get up at a certain time.” All the while keep an image of that time in your mind. In this way you make yourself really understand that you will be getting up at that time. Then, after sleeping you will get up at exactly the time you wanted to. As your health becomes better, this ability will become more and more accurate.

2
Dreams of Heaven

From time immemorial, people have looked to the heavens for signs and portents of the future. Celestial events such as comets, falling stars, and eclipses, whether appearing in dreams or in reality, have long been thought to presage events on earth.

Now let us see how celestial phenomena can appear in dreams and how we can interpret them.

1. If you see yourself going toward heaven, or flying in a cloud, or going up and up, this is a good dream. You will have progress. You will become successful. This is a very good dream.

2. If, however, you see yourself going down, falling from a cliff or the clouds, this is a bad dream. You will meet with failure.

3. If, when you are falling down, instead of falling rapidly, you fall slowly, that is better than the rapid fall.

4. As you know, at the extremes, everything changes into its opposite. If you see a dream of yourself flying higher and higher, to extreme heights, this is a bad dream. Your success will be too great, and you will fall back to the earth.

5. If there is light in the dream, if the dream is bright, with light or sunshine, then the dream is a good one. Your future will be bright.

6. If, however, the dream is full of darkness and mist, the

dream is a bad one. It does not bode well.

7. If light begins to appear in the mist or clouds, this dream indicates that in the beginning you will face difficulties, but soon after you will become happy.

8. If a bright dream begins to become clouded or dark, then your present happiness and good fortune will soon be in peril.

9. When you see the sun, it shows your future direction, or your future in general. If the sun is bright, then your future will be bright. If the sun is pale and wan, then your future is dim.

10. When you see the moon, it shows your emotional relations with other people. If the moon is bright, then you will become happy and merry. If the moon is sad, then your relations with other people will also become sad.

11. You may see the stars in your dreams. One star is showing yourself. It will usually be a bright and shining star. Many stars usually indicate your many friends and relatives.

12. If you see meteors or comets, these indicate how your future will go on, or how events go on. If these celestial bodies travel smoothly with a long tail, this is a good dream.

13. If, however, these celestial bodies float around without a clear direction, that is not a good sign.

14. If you see a meteor that keeps falling without end, this is not a good sign.

15. If, however, the meteor or comet comes down to earth and turns into a rock or mountain, this shows that you are becoming materially and socially stable.

16. When you see a rainbow it indicates whether you have a colorful life or not. A colorful rainbow shows a colorful future.

17. If, instead of a seven-colored rainbow, you see a white rainbow, that is not good. It is better to see a rainbow with colors.

18. If the rainbow is big and clear, this is a good sign.

19. A dim rainbow that quickly disappears is only a fair sign.

20. When you see the Milky Way in your dreams, it indicates separation from your parents, from your family, from

your friends. A separation or divorce may arise. Or you may go on a long journey leaving your family behind.

21. When you see snow in your dreams, it indicates your social environment. If plenty of snow is falling, that is a good sign—you have many friends. Big flakes are also a good omen.

22. However, if only a few flurries of snow are falling, that indicates you have only a few friends.

23. If a blizzard appears, it indicates many social changes.

24. If the scene of snow includes animals, especially carnivorous animals like wolves, bears, or tigers, that is a bad omen. Someone near you, a friend or a relative, may have an accident.

25. If you see plant-eating animals like deer or rabbits in the snow scene, that is a better dream. Your human relations are much more peaceful.

26. When you see frost in your dreams, this indicates a lack of clarity. It is a bad omen. You will have many doubts and wonders.

27. In the dream of frost, if the frost melts away, this is a good sign. Your doubts are vanishing, and you will be able to see your future clearly.

28. When you see thunder and lightning in your dreams, this indicates that you are making some kind of determination. There is a self-revolution coming about. There is a change in your self-determination.

29. Rain in your dreams indicates a clarification of confusion.

30. If, however, you are caught in a driving rain and you get soaked, this is a bad dream. It indicates that you are caught in great confusion.

31. There is another interesting dream related to rain: you and your sweetheart are walking in the rain under one umbrella; this dream indicates separation. If you and your sweetheart are walking together but there is no rain, perhaps you are walking in the sun, or under the moon, that is a good dream; but under the rain, that is a bad sign; it is an omen of separation.

What kind of person sees the sun? A more yang type of

person. The heart is the organ associated with the sun. What kind of person sees the moon? A yin type of person. The lungs are the organ associated with the moon.

When you see certain symbols in your dreams, try to reflect upon which organs are affected, and what foods you ate to produce this effect. You remember that yesterday you ate an orange or a piece of banana, this affected your lungs and made you emotional. You had an emotional dream, and naturally you are going to be emotional in your waking life. So you are still in the same frame of mind in your waking life that you had when the dream took place. That is why there is such a close connection between a true dream and the daily life in which you live. The dream is only indicating to you what to expect of your life because of the condition of your internal organs. You will act in the same manner as your dream indicated because your physical condition is still the same.

What part of the body is associated with a dream of stars? The body cells. The food which will produce a true dream of stars is one which is full of protein, either animal protein or vegetable protein—such as beans. But if the protein contains more mineral salts, then you will see the sun. If you take more liquid, then you will see the dream of rain or mist or even frost. The dream of a rainbow will come if you are eating vegetables, the more colorful the vegetables, the more colorful the dream.

The various dreams of heaven, and their general interpretations, are summarized on the following page.

Table 1
Dreams of Heaven

Image	Positive	Negative
Flying or falling	You going toward heaven	You falling to earth
Light or darkness	Bright light or sunshine	Darkness or mist
Sun	Strong bright sunshine	Pale or weak sun
Moon	A bright happy moon	A dim or sad moon
Stars	One or many bright stars	The Milky Way galaxy
Comets or meteors	Comets with a clear direction	Comets moving aimlessly
Rainbow	A colorful rainbow	A white, dim, or fading rainbow
Snow	Heavy snow	Light flurries
Frost	Melting frost	Scene of frost
Rain	Scene of rain	Getting caught in heavy rain

3
Dreams of Earth

There are many phenomena on the earth, like mountains, rivers, oceans, rocks, stones, fields, trees, and flowers. All of these can be seen as symbols in your dreams. They are projections of your thinking, your memory, and your imagination. Now let us see what these images mean.

1. When you see a mountain in your dream, this indicates your life direction. If you are climbing the mountain, this is a good dream. It shows progress in the direction of your life.

2. If the top of the mountain is covered with clouds, this shows that you do not know where you are going. Yes, you are going, but you do not know where.

3. If the mountain suddenly starts to crumble, great trouble in the direction of your life will begin. You may experience some type of loss or confusion.

4. While your are climbing the mountain, if you finally reach the top, this is a bad dream. This is a sign that you have no place to go but down.

5. While you are going up the mountain, if you can see the top clearly, but then clouds come, or mist, and thunder sounds, and you can no longer see the mountain clearly, this is a sign that you will become sick. You are becoming physi-

cally and mentally weak. The mountain represents your ideal.

6. When you see a river (you may either see the river, or be on a boat on the river), this indicates the course of events in your life. If the river has many curves, this indicates that there will be complications in your daily life routine.

7. If the river is flowing smoothly, then the course of your daily life will run smoothly.

8. If you see fish in the river, these indicate your friends or the people who are around you. The number of fish indicates the number of friends who are around you, or the amount of time during which the event involving the friends will continue.

9. Whenever you see a rock, especially a big rock that is strong and unmovable, that is a sign of stability and safety. Seeing rocks in your dreams is a good sign.

10. If you see a rock, and the rock suddenly collapses or falls down from a mountain, this indicates that the foundation of whatever you are now doing is shaky. You can expect bad events.

11. If you see stones or pebbles in your dream, this indicates the objects that surround you—your money, your wealth, your possessions.

12. Plenty of stones point to the accumulation of plenty of material wealth. But if you see great masses of stones, this is a bad sign. You will be accumulating too much material wealth, and this indicates the beginning of your becoming poor. Stones or pebbles are best gathered one-by-one. This shows that your progress is slow and steady.

13. If the stones are brightly colored, this indicates good fortune.

14. When you see the ocean in your dreams, this indicates that there is too much water in the body cells, especially the brain cells, and the body is literally drowning in excess liquid. This shows that the kidneys are affected.

15. When you see water surrounding you and making you suffer, that is a sign of sickness and misfortune.

16. If you see the water from the outside or from above, for example, if you are standing on the beach, and there is no suffering involved, this is often a good sign, a sign of good for-

tune. The ocean symbolizes your future.

17. If you are going on a boat or ship upon the ocean, that dream shows the course of your life. If a hurricane suddenly arises and you and the boat are sunk, this shows that in the near future you will experience many difficulties.

18. If you see a hurricane on the ocean, that means your intestines are in trouble as well as your sinuses.

19. Let us consider flowers. If you see a beautiful flower on the field, the size of the flower is important. Flowers symbolize your mentality. A small flower is good—this indicates a humble nature.

20. A large extravagant flower indicates arrogance and pride. If you see a garden full of flowers, this is not good, misfortune will arise.

21. If you see a butterfly above the flower, this shows that your human relations will be difficult, especially the sexual ones. There may be extramarital affairs.

22. If you see just the butterfly and not the flower, then this indicates that your mind is floating. It cannot be fixed on any one thing. It is is sign of instability, or the inability to make up your mind.

23. If you see fields in your dreams, different interpretations can be given. If you are walking in the field alone, this is a good dream. You are working toward what you want to have.

24. If you are walking together with your sweetheart on the field, this is a bad dream. It is a sign of separation. It may appear to be an intimate, romantic dream, but the result is opposite.

25. If you see yourself planting the field, this is a good sign; a woman who sees such a dream will bear a healthy and strong child.

26. If you are walking on the field and suddenly an earthquake arises, this is a bad dream; it is a dream of misfortune.

27. If the earthquake causes a hole to appear in front of you and you are not swallowed up, then you will escape the misfortune. But if the hole swallows you up, you will be overcome by misfortune.

28. If you see plenty of trees—a forest—different interpretations can be given:

Pine or cedar trees indicate a good position.

Willow trees indicate sickness or misfortune, a depressed mental condition.

Bamboo trees indicate a successful course of events.

Birch trees indicate that generally everything is all right.

Maple trees indicate a wishy-washy condition.

29. A jungle indicates that a present problem is too complicated, especially if you see yourself in the jungle. But if you see the jungle from the outside or from above, then this is a better sign.

30. A trail through the forest is a good sign; it shows a path through your present problems.

When you see stones, mountains, forests, and other natural objects, these things are symbolic. They represent other things which are part of our imagination. But these images reveal what we are thinking about. This is the movie or film of your thoughts, and you are the movie director. Or you are the painter with an empty canvas, and you are creating a painting with your imagination. You create what you want to see. You bring into vivid life those things about which you are thinking.

When you see a dream, remember that it reflects your condition. By your dreams you can judge, examine, and review your sickness or your general condition. If you are troubled, then your organs are troubled and that causes your mentality to be troubled. Once we understand this, then we can interpret our dreams and understand exactly which organs require attention in order for our bodies to be healthy.

The various dreams of earth and natural phenomena are summarized on the following page.

Table 2
Dreams of Earth

Image	Positive	Negative
Mountains	You climbing a mountain	You at the top of a mountain
Rivers	River flowing in a straight course	River flowing in a complicated course
Rocks	A large unmovable rock	The rock collapses or falls down
Stones or pebbles	You gathering stones one-by-one	A large pile of stones or pebbles
Ocean	The ocean from a distance	You surrounded by the ocean
Flowers	A small flower	A large extravagant flower
Fields	You walking alone in a field	You walking in a field with your loved-one
Trees	Pine, cedar, bamboo, or birch	Willow or maple trees
Forest	A trail through a forest	You surrounded by jungle or forest

4
Dreams of Humanity

Dreams of humanity are the dreams of persons, or those in which people appear.

1. If you see people such as nobles, or spiritual people, or a sage or a saint, these indicate a good dream. They represent something good that is about to happen.

2. If you see a priest or a monk, this is a bad dream because these people are the ones who take care of funerals. It may be a sign of your own funeral. This is especially true of a dream in which you are walking with the priest or monk. This is a bad dream. Be careful.

3. If you see yourself developing an infirmity in a dream,, for example no longer being able to walk or to see, this is a sign that you will be accused of something. Someone is about to make a complaint about you.

4. If you see a thief in your dream, it indicates that you are thinking about money, otherwise you would not be seeing a thief. There are two interpretations about thieves:

If the thief loves you, this is a good sign for your future.
If the thief does not love you, this is a bad sign.

When you are in a deep sleep, your so-called conscience,

or judgment of good and bad, is working well. While you are awake you may be selfish and egocentric, but while you are sleeping that selfishness and egocentricity may disappear. You may be thinking about your possessions and you see the dream of a thief. At that time, if a robbery occurs, it is actually a good thing. Your conscience is seeing that. The thief is simply removing your excess.

5. If you see in your dream a woman, she represents three different things:

She represents the home, or care of the home and the people in it.

She represents sexual desire.

She represents the spending of money.

6. If you see a man in your dream, he also represents three things:

He represents power.

He represents the sexual drive.

He represents fighting and competition.

7. If you see a naked man or a naked woman in your dream is that a good or a bad dream? If there is no erotic feeling, this is a good dream; it is a dream of admiration for the opposite sex.

8. If you see a naked member of the opposite sex and the dream is accompanied by sexual feelings, this is a sign that you may soon be having a quarrel or argument with your sweetheart or spouse. This will happen because you have too much vitality, so that in the daytime your attitude may be too domineering—so the quarrel may arise.

9. If you see a dream of sexual intercourse, several interpretations can be given. If you are involved in the scene (you are having intercourse), the physical cause of this kind of dream is overeating, especially protein and fat. This dream is a sign that in the near future you will be involved in human troubles. You may have a quarrel or argument. It is also a sign of spending too much money because of frustration.

Spending money, at least fifty percent of the time, is caused by sexual frustration. Spring is the mating season; at that time new sales in stores goes up.

10. If you see the dream of sexual intercourse, but you are not involved in it, in fact, you may not even know any of the people involved in the act, this is an indication that you are a cautious person, that you are controlling yourself. Yet there is stagnation. Your conscience is controlling your feelings of desire.

11. If you see the dream of two persons making love, and your sweetheart is one of them, this is a sign that you are going to quarrel, and perhaps separate. There may be jealousy involved.

12. If you have a dream of a dead person, this may be a good dream, especially if the person comes to life and talks to you. Your seeing an image of the person evidences your love and care for that person.

13. However, if you see a deceased person in your dream, and that person asks you to come along with him or her, this is a bad sign. It may indicate that you will have an accident that could cause your death.

14. If you see a dream in which you are bowing to your friend or your senior, so that you are surrendering yourself to your friend, this is a good sign. It indicates that you will become a great person, you will have success, your position will be increased.

15. However, if you see a dream in which your friend or senior is bowing to you, this is a bad sign. Soon your position will be lost, you will lose your position.

True dreams involving people are summarized on the following page.

Table 3
Dreams of Humanity

Positive Images	Negative Images
Nobles or spiritual people	A priest or monk; You walking with a priest or monk
A friendly thief	An unfriendly thief
A member of the opposite sex unaccompanied by sexual feelings	A member of the opposite sex accompanied by sexual feelings; You or your sweetheart involved in intercourse
A deceased person who begins talking to you	A deceased person who invites you to come with him
You bowing to your friend or senior	Your friend or senior bowing to you

5
Miscellaneous Dreams

The three categories of dreams that we studied so far did not include images of animals. Let us investigate the symbolism of animals that appear in dreams.

1. If you see a dream in which you are riding on a horse, this is a symbol that you are soon going to have difficulties.

2. If you see in your dream a cow or ox, this is a symbol of your success, you will be successful.

3. If you see a dog in your dream, this is a sign of quarreling, or conflicts with other people.

4. If you see a cat in your dream, this shows your material goods. A sleeping cat indicates material stability.

5. If you see an agitated cat in your dream that is an indication of material instability.

6. If you see a black cat in your dream, it is a sign of bad luck.

7. If you see a tiger in your dream, this is a sign of power and dignity. If a woman sees a tiger in her dream, she will bear a noble child. If a man sees a tiger in his dream, this indicates that his position will become powerful and dignified.

8. If you see a lion in your dream (you may either see the lion or be riding on the lion), this indicates that your position

will develop into a mighty and powerful one.

9. If you see a sparrow in your dream, this indicates unexpected visitors. The number of sparrows shows either the number of visitors or the number of days until the visitors arrive.

10. If you see a chicken or a rooster in your dream, this is a bad sign. Bad things will happen.

11. If you see a pheasant in your dream, this symbolizes that you are going to have good things happen to you.

12. If you see a cockroach in your dream, this is a sign that your household will collapse.

13. If you see a mouse or rat in your dream, this is a sign that your household will prosper.

14. If you see a dragonfly in your dream, this is a sign that people will trust you.

15. If you see a centipede in your dream, this indicates that your financial situation will improve; you will gain profit.

Table 4
Dreams of Animals and Insects

Positive Images	Negative Images
Cow or ox	You riding a horse
Sleeping cat	Black cat
Tiger	Agitated cat
Lion	Dog
Pheasant	Chicken or rooster
Mouse	Cockroach
Rat	
Dragonfly	
Centipede	

Miscellaneous Dreams

In this type of dream, there are four general categories, even though they may be combined:

Dreams Concerning Food and Drink This kind of dream concerns your health and sickness.

Dreams of Events If the event is a party or a social occasion, then this is a good sign, a sign of good luck. If the event is a funeral, this is a bad sign, a sign of bad luck. These events generally indicate the course of your life. You may also see yourself performing certain actions. When you see events, the yang events are generally good. The yin events are generally bad. A funeral is a yin event, it is a bad dream. A party is a yang event, it is a good dream.

Dreams of Household Tools and Furnishings If the tools are properly used, then this is a good dream. If the tools are improperly used, then this is a bad dream. This kind of dream generally indicates your daily life.

Dreams of Moving Things These include dreams of cars, trains, and airplanes. If the movement is rapid, then the dream is a bad one. If the movement is steady, or if there is no movement at all, then the dream is a good one. This kind of dream indicates the movement of your life or your direction.

Now let us examine several examples of the above.

1. If you see yourself enjoying food in the company of other people, this is a happy dream. Your life will become better.

2. If you see a dream in which you are eating candy, fruit, or ice cream, this is a bad dream. Soon you will have to face difficulties. You could become sick.

3. If you see a dream in which you are eating alone, this is a bad sign. You will soon become sick. The one exception to this interpretation is if you see yourself in the dream eating diet number seven (one hundred percent whole grains); then it is a good sign.

4. If you see in your dream that you are changing your clothes to new ones, this is a sign that you are going to change your environment. Garments, clothes, jewelry all indicate your environment. You may change your job. You may move to another city. Some kind of change will take place.

5. If you see in your dream that you are changing your socks and shoes, this means that you are going to change the

place of your residence. You may move into another apartment or house, or from one city to another.

6. If you see in your dream that you are reading a book or writing poetry or a novel, this is a good sign. It indicates your diligence and steadfastness.

7. If you see in your dream that you are writing a farewell letter, this is a bad dream. It indicates that there will soon be a separation, perhaps even a divorce.

8. If you see in your dream that your hair is falling out, this is a bad sign. You will lose your fortune, your property, your goods. You may even become sick.

9. If you see in a dream that your teeth are falling out, this is a bad sign. If there is a sick person in the family or maybe among your friends, this person could possibly die. To see in the dream that you are losing your molars indicates the possible loss of a member of your immediate family.

10. If you see in the dream that you are playing cards or playing chess or betting on horses, and you win, this is a bad sign. This dream can also be applied to passing an examination. Winning is too flamboyant.

11. If you see in your dream that you are taking an examination, but you have failed, this is a better dream. It indicates your modesty and carefulness.

12. If you see in the dream that you are flying in the air, this is a bad sign. It is a sign of sickness or an accident.

13. If you see a fire in your dream, several interpretations can be given. If you or your friends or family are involved, then this fire may actually occur, so be careful.

14. However, if you see a fire but no one is involved, then this is a good sign. All delusions will disappear. A new life will occur with a burning desire and a new ideal.

15. If you see in your dream that you are going to a ceremony, if the ceremony is one of worship, then this is a good sign.

16. If, on the other hand, you see yourself going to a funeral, this is a bad sign. It is also a sign that you will soon be spending money.

17. If you see in your dream that you are going into the kitchen, this means that soon you will receive an invitation

to a dinner or a delicious meal.

18. If you see in your dream a clock or a watch, two interpretations may be given:

You may be late, or miss an important appointment.
Some unusual guest will come to visit you.

19. If you see pots and pans and dishes in your dream, these symbolize that your home is stable; your financial status is stable.

20. If you see a broken mirror in your dream, this is a bad sign. Someone near to you may die or become sick, or you yourself may become sick or have an accident.

21. If you see in your dream that you are doing carpentry work, this is a good sign.

22. If you have a dream in which you are digging out a well, or doing plumbing work, or digging a water channel, this is a good dream. You are planning your future; you can have a good stable future.

23. If you see in your dream that you are working with knives and tools, this is also a good dream. If you see yourself holding the knife, this is a good sign.

24. If you see someone else holding a knife, that is also all right. But if you see yourself giving a knife to someone else, that is a bad dream. You may lose your position. You may lose your possessions. You may lose a friendship with someone.

25. If you see in the dream that you are traveling in a car or on a train, this indicates that whatever you are now doing will be postponed. Plans are going to extend indefinitely. There will be no conclusion. More time is necessary.

26. If you see in your dream that you are riding on a bicycle, this indicates that whatever you are doing will develop smoothly.

27. If you see an automobile in your dream, several conclusions can be reached. If the automobile is stopped, this indicates that whatever you are now doing will be accomplished.

28. If, however, the automobile is moving, this indicates that whatever you are expecting will not be accomplished.

29. If you see an airplane, several possibilities arise. If the

airplane is flying over water, this is a good sign. It indicates happiness.

30. If, however, the airplane is flying amidst the clouds, this is a bad sign. It is a sign that you will have difficulties.

These miscellaneous dreams are summarized in the following table.

Table 5
Miscellaneous Dreams

Positive Images	Negative Images
Eating with others	Eating alone
Reading or writing	Eating candy or ice cream
Failing an examination	Writing a farewell letter
Going to a ceremony of worship	Teeth or hair falling out
Going into a kitchen	Winning at gambling
Pots and pans	Flying in the air
Doing carpentry work	A fire in which friends or family are involved
Working with tools	Going to a funeral
Holding a knife	A broken mirror
Riding on a bicycle	Handing a knife to someone
A stationary car	Traveling in a car or train
An airplane flying over water	A moving car
A fire in which you, your family, or friends are not involved	An airplane flying in clouds
Doing plumbing work or digging a water channel	

6
Food and Dreams

Most true dreams fall into the categories presented in the previous chapters. These interpretations can help you understand what the signs or symbols in your dreams mean. If the dream is a bad one, full of bad signs, then you can start to change yourself. You can heal the organs which are out of balance, so that your body will become better and your mentality will become better. You can do this by changing your diet.

Your dreams are nothing more than the mental images produced by the state of health of your organs. Ill health may appear as diarrhea in the body, but in the mind this ill health appears as bad dreams. Both the physical and the mental manifestations of ill health can be eliminated by curing the condition of the internal organs.

Usually people do not realize that they are creating their own dreams. They are not conscious of their own ability to determine their dream. They just think that the dream is speaking to them. They regard the dream as an omen, as a means of fortune telling. But this is just the opposite of what dreams really are. Dreams are a reflection of the condition of the internal organs. When you have an upset stomach, you would be wise to see what you had been eating that caused it. In the same way, you can determine from your dreams that you had been eating something wrong which upset one of your organs, thus producing a bad dream.

Most people do not know that when they have a bad dream, it was caused by an upset organ. They do not realize that the bad dream was caused by something they ate. When wise people see a bad dream, however, they understand what caused it. They then begin a systematic change of their diet to correct the imbalance.

Our dreams have a quality that is similar to our thoughts during the day. We have the same feelings and imagination during our waking hours that we do while asleep. If our dreams are dark, depressing, or frightening, then during the day we will also be frightened, depressed, or have dark feelings. This comes from what we are eating. As soon as you awake in the morning after having a dream, think about what it was you ate the day before that may have caused it.

For thousands of years, people have tried to interpret their dreams. They have tried to use dreams to foretell the future. These interpretations are sometimes accurate because when a person has certain dreams, it is possible to know why those dreams appear. What a person eats determines the quality of his blood and the quality of his brain. He will think and act in a certain way that is determined by his diet. Dreams are an accurate reflection of our health and even our destiny.

The understanding of dreams therefore makes it possible to predict what will happen to someone, unless, of course, he changes his way of eating and way of life. If you understand this well, then you can eat in a certain way in order to see a specific dream. If you want to see your sweetheart in a dream, you can eat certain foods or try a certain style of cooking so as to see him or her that night. It is also possible to recommend certain dishes for the specific type of dream you want: nightmares, romantic dreams, fragmentary dreams, or a dream in which you see the future. It is possible to make dietary recommendations for about forty or fifty kinds of dreams. The key to this ability is to understand the relationship between food and dreams.

I studied this relationship by studying my own dreams.

After I knew macrobiotics and the importance of the order of the universe, I started to correlate my dreams with what I had eaten the day before. I kept a diary. I did this for many years. Then it became clear. In order to confirm this, I would eat again several days later the food I thought had caused the dream. That night I would have the same, or a similar dream. In that way, I confirmed my conclusions. You can also study your dreams in this manner.

I studied Oriental diagnosis in the same way, by actually experiencing it. I was in New York, twenty-four or twenty-five years old, standing on Fifth Avenue or riding in the subway. Every day I saw faces. One week, I looked at noses only. The next week, I studied ears. The following week, I observed eyes. Do you know how many pairs of eyes you can see in one week in New York? So many. In that way I learned diagnosis. Self-training is important. Through it you can understand more and more.

Yin and Yang Dreams

Among dreams there are certain basic or fundamental ones. Basic dreams are closer to true dreams and come from our desire to live as a human being. They are a reflection of our genuine, native consciousness. For example, when you are hungry or when you fast, you have a dream of food. Or if you are thirsty, you dream of water. Cravings for food appear often in dreams. Also in this category are dreams of sex, or dreams in which you seek your parents, children, or home. When you do not have these things, you create them in your dreams. For example, if a woman does not conceive after several years of trying, she may dream about having a baby. Or when their children move far away, parents may see them in their dreams. Dreams such as this are common. Everyone has them.

I did not have dreams of food until I became a soldier and did not eat for three days, during which time I worked hard. After only twenty minutes of sleep, I would start to dream of food. These dreams revealed my innermost desires. Unless you face hunger, poverty, and difficulty, you may not have such dreams. It is only when you face such situations that basic dreams appear.

The dreams we have at night are not different from those we see during the day. During the day you may see and desire certain things but you pretend not to. At night however, these inner feelings come out. People usually refer to these inner, hidden desires as the subconscious. But it is more accurate to refer to them as our real consciousness. These inner feelings are based on our desire to continue living. Our daily, surface consciousness is actually our subconscious.

Like everything else, dreams can be classified according to yin and yang.

Suppose you have a dream in which you are separated from your friend or lover or are going far away. Which category of dream is that? It is a more yin dream. Opposite to that are dreams in which you approach or come closer to your loved-ones or friends. These are more yang dreams. Suppose you see yourself swimming in the ocean, far from the shore or far from your home. Which category is this? Yin. On the other hand, active, exciting, and happy dreams are yang. If you see yourself dropping or losing something, that is a yin dream. If you see someone giving you something, or if you win the lottery, that is a yang dream. Seeing your hair or teeth falling out is more yin.

If you see a star in your dream, and it is a dim, solitary star, that is a more yin dream. If you see a bright star, that is a yang dream. If you see the moon and it is dim, your condition is yin. If the moon is bright, your condition is more yang.

Dreams of water are yin; dreams of fire are yang. If you see yourself drowning, your condition is yin. Your bloodstream and brain are full of water. Your dream is a reflection of your condition. Similarly, if you see a lake, ocean, or river, these images represent a yin condition caused by your intake of liquid. On the contrary, if you see a dream of fire, it means your condition is more yang. Your body vibration is flaming. Dreams of fire can be caused by fever or from too much animal food. They also result from alcohol and spices.

Dreams of suffocation have several causes. Too much liquid can produce an image of drowning or suffocation by water. Mucus deposits in the lungs caused by cheese, milk, and other dairy foods can also create an image of suffocation. Interestingly, we often make up stories to justify our condition. Perhaps you remember during childhood having had dreams of someone pressing on your chest, so that you were choking. You may have imagined that another person was pressing on you but in reality, that dream was a reflection of your own condition. Your imagination developed as a result of your condition.

Similarly, you may have had dreams in which you fell down and part of your body became paralyzed. As a result, you were unable to move or cry. When you woke up, you discovered that your arm was asleep. You made up a story in your imagination. The causes were real, but the story was made up. As we can see, dreams have some basis in reality.

Dreams of flying have a more yang cause. More yang birds eat insects, small mammals, and small grains or seeds. They are able to fly to great heights. Domesticated chickens or turkeys, which are yin, are unable to fly. In a similar way, people who are able to perform levitation are yang. They eat a more yang diet and practice more yang forms of meditation in which they concentrate their energy. If you eat and drink plenty, your condition becomes yin and you prefer sitting to standing. When you are lighter, you are more attracted to standing up and being active. People who are yang have a tendency to walk upward on their toes.

Among so-called nightmares, there are two types. In one, you are being tortured, attacked, or chased. So you are frightened, trying to run away. The other type is bloody. You are joining in the killing, murdering, or war. One type is passive, the other, more active. What is the cause of the passive type of nightmare? Extreme yin, such as sugar and alcohol, together with meat and animal food.

Active nightmares have a yang cause: they are caused almost entirely by meat and animal food. For example, in Western movies, there is often a lot of gun-fighting and killing. Whenever there is a scene of the characters eating, they are almost always eating meat. And so they fight and kill each other over minor incidents. They are seeing daymares. A person who has nightmares also sees daymares when he is awake.

If you see the world as chaotic, regardless of whether you see this dream during the day or at night, what kind of food are you eating? This dream is one of confusion and chaos. Nowadays, people think the world is chaotic and in crisis, and that society is declining. Why do such feelings arise? Is the world really in crisis? If you think and act as if the world situation is critical, a world crisis will definitely come. If we visualize a certain dream and act according to it, it can easily become reality.

For example, if you have antagonistic feelings toward your parents and think they cannot understand you, you have a certain dream or vision of them. In reality, they may love you, but you may be unable to see this and so you think they are bad. Then you act that way. You run away from home. You do not write. You tell your friends, "My parents are bad." When you find a partner, you do not tell your parents. Because of the image you have created, in reality you become more and more separate from them. Your dream creates your reality. In the same way, if someone says the stock market is about to fall, people start whispering, the rumor spreads, and eventually they begin selling their stocks. As a result, the market falls. Vision creates action.

Why do we see dreams of chaos? The order of the universe never changes, regardless of whether the earth or solar system ends. Even if an entirely new universe comes into being, the order of the universe continues. The real dream is not chaos. If we see chaos, something is wrong with us.

We need to eat in an orderly way, both in terms of proportions and cooking. If you eat in a disorderly way, for example, no grains as principal foods, or if you eat more side dishes than main dishes, or you begin with dessert, then vegetables, then grains—upside-down eating—then you see a chaotic dream. If you would like to see a chaotic dream, then please eat this way. Then you will feel a sense of crisis and urgency.

When you see a dream of flooding, the cause is too much liquid. The brain is watery so you start to see a flood. When I speak about the earth's axis having shifted in the past, and a great flood arising, some people think this will happen again in several years and want to know to where to move in order to be safe. They may have dreams of floods. These dreams are caused by too much liquid.

As we saw earlier, dreams of fire are often caused by spices. Spices make you feel hot. Among common foods, pizza gives you a hot, burning feeling and can cause you to have a dream of fire. Any food that causes the tongue or mouth to become hot can make you dream of fire.

Dreams of sex, especially active sex, are caused by eating too much, especially too much protein. Sex is a fundamental, basic desire. It correlates with the eating of primary life forms. If you eat various kinds of invertebrates, including shellfish, squid, and octopus, or eggs, including caviar, you may have sexual dreams. Eggs are a primordial form of food.

Dreams of falling are caused by eating too many tree fruits—such as apples or pears, or foods such as coconuts. These are more yin dreams, and may indicate an irregular heart beat.

Dreams of anxiety and worry may arise from time to time. During certain periods, you feel more comfortable, while at other times, you may experience feelings of anxiety, both during the day and at night. Your anxiety may continue for one day, several days, or a few weeks. What is the cause of such anxiety? When you become anxious, you do not have a harmonious, settled-down feeling. Worry and anxiety occur when your combination of food becomes out of balance. If the combination of foods is really bad, then you become toxic. If the combination is not too bad, yet not so good, feelings of anxiety come—an unsettled feeling. If you eat plenty of grains, you do not feel this much. If the combination of side dishes is out of balance, then you feel anxiety. If you change the order in your diet, in several days, anxiety will disappear.

Dreams of sickness, for example, lung conditions such as pneumonia, asthma, or bronchitis, are caused by cold foods and liquids. By itself, water does not cause such dreams to appear, but cold water or liquid—including iced drinks—can make these dreams happen.

Many people see dreams of separation or divorce. What causes a dream such as this? Extremely yin foods have the potential to make us see this kind of dream. Examples include tomatoes, ice cream, fruit (especially tropical fruit), sugar, too much oil, artificial vinegar, additives and preservatives, potatoes, white flour, and spices. Foods such as these can cause our thinking to become fragmented. Refined, partial foods in general have this potential, in comparison to whole foods that cause our thinking to become more unified.

Dreams of quarreling are caused by animal food, including steak, hamburger, and frankfurters. Excess salt contributes to these dreams, as do strongly yang varieties of fish, such as bluefish, swordfish, and tuna. When you eat a steak made from these types of fish, you become very yang. The meat is often hard. If you eat these things together with salt or shoyu, you may become angry and quarrel. Dreams of quarrelling are caused by too much salt plus animal food, regardless of whether meat or fish.

In a dream of war, the quarrelling is stronger and more urgent. War is more universal, explosive, and fiery. The basis for dreams of war is strong yang: meat and animal food. What causes the underlying tension produced by meat-eating to erupt into violence? Spices. Meat and spices, poultry and spices, and fish and spices—those are the direct causes of war. Sugar and chemicalized foods contribute, but are not the main cause. In the case of European countries, which have had many more wars than countries in Asia, the cause is a high intake of meat and other forms of animal food. If we change our food, everyone will start to become more peaceful.

In some dreams, a person may start to dislike their husband or wife, or boyfriend or girlfriend. In other words, they start to dislike the opposite sex. Dreams such as this are often caused by eating figs. Figs cause us to lose interest in sex. They can inhibit conception and cause miscarriage. If you eat figs every day, you may start to think of becoming a nun or a priest. In the Orient there is a proverb stating that if you have a fig tree in your backyard, your home will decline and you will have no offspring. This folk wisdom is not based on superstition, but on thousands of years of experience. Figs are purple and cold to the touch—very yin. Whatever is so yin tastes delicious because, as human beings, we are yang. Strong yin vegetables such as eggplant, mushroom, and asparagus can also cause dreams such as these. When eaten excessively, these vegetables can make a person dislike sex.

Dreams of attachment, in which someone does something to you and you cannot forget it, or in which you lose something and cannot forget about it, are caused by sticky foods. Sticky, greasy dishes like pizza and casseroles contribute to dreams such as these. When you eat dishes in which many ingredients are mixed-up, you often do not know what foods you are eating. These dishes create a condition of sticky attachment.

Dreams of traveling by sea are caused by eating fish and seafood, especially invertebrates such as shellfish. Dreams of traveling in an airplane result from drinking coffee. Dreams of traveling on land are the product of eating dried foods like raisins or dried sea vegetables.

Exotic, ethnic foods cause a variety of exotic dreams. If you go to a Middle Eastern restaurant and eat a meal, that night you may dream of *A Thousand and One Arabian Nights*. If you eat Chinese food, you may have a dream about Chinese history. If you eat ethnic food, you often see dreams of adventure and fables from those countries. If you would like to write exciting adventure stories, please eat at exotic restaurants.

As we can see, when we eat more yin types of food, we see yin dreams. When we eat more yang types of food, we see more yang dreams. These dreams appear during the day and at night. When we eat in a more balanced manner, we start to see true dreams. Then our dream of life starts to change and our vision of the world becomes healthy and peaceful. If one person in the world carries a true dream, the whole world is encouraged. If more people share the dream, then the world can be changed. By your dream you encourage all other people who may be dreaming illusory dreams. They will understand and be encouraged. Then your words will carry true spirit.

Let us change our condition so we see only true dreams. When you want to do something, find out what kind of food you need to eat. Then you will automatically become like that. Great people in the past did not know what made them great. They did not create themselves. Although in many ways they were great, they were still slaves to the order of the universe. Now that you know the secret that creates such ability, such people, you can use it to direct and orient your life. That means you are a free person.

The relationship between food and common dreams is summarized in the following table.

Table 6
Relationship Between Food and Dreams

Type of Dream	Dietary Cause
Confusion and chaos	Disorderly eating
Flooding	Too much liquid
Fire	Spicy food
Sex	Primordial food
Falling	Tree fruits
Anxiety and worry	Disharmony of food
Sickness in lungs	Cold liquid
Separation or divorce	Yin extremes
Quarrelling	Salt plus animal food
War	Spices plus animal food
Dislike of opposite sex	Figs
Attachment	Sticky, greasy food
Traveling by sea	Invertebrates
Traveling by airplane	Coffee
Traveling on land	Dried foods (fruits, sea vegetables)

Creating Your Dream

It is important to understand that we are the creators of our dreams. The kind of dream you see is determined by what you are eating. Yes, there is a certain amount of vibration from the infinite universe which will influence the kind of dream you will have. But, for the most part, your dreams are determined by what you take in. By changing the quality of what you take in, you change the quality of your dreams. The ability to determine your own dream is the state of the free person. When you become a free person, then you can really say that you are a macrobiotic person. Before that you are just a macrobiotic student.

A macrobiotic student knows how certain foods produce certain results. Thus, he can use food to influence whatever he wants. But, the macrobiotic person is able to take any kind of food, or any combination of foods, or any type of cooking, in order to see a certain dream, in order to do something. For that purpose he or she can select the type of food he or she wants. That is really free eating.

There are seven levels of eating:

1. Spontaneous or Mechanical Eating This level of eating can be summarized as follows: "I am hungry, therefore I will go to the kitchen and eat whatever is there." Many people eat this way. Many people are going to the kitchen for a midnight snack and just eating because they are hungry. There is no thought at all about the food, or what the food will do to the body; there is no concern about the nourishment or lack of nourishment it will cause; there is no thought about how many times the food needs to be chewed. It is just spontaneous gratification of the pang of hunger. Practically ninety percent of people are eating at this level.

2. Sensory Eating This level of eating can be summarized by the thought: "This food looks delicious, it smells nice, therefore I want to eat it." People who stare in the window of pastry shops eyeing the cream puffs and eclairs are caught in the sensory level of eating. They are attracted to the taste or appearance of the food. They still have no concern for the nutritional quality of the food, only its attractiveness.

Advertising takes advantage of the sensory level. If food is packaged in an attractive wrapper, if it is presented to the public with an attractive commercial or catchy slogan, it will sell well. If people could get beyond the sensory level of eating, then the large food marketing companies would collapse. The people who are caught in the sensory level are the supporters of big industry.

3. Sentimental or Emotional Eating Ethnic cooking falls into this category. Many people who immigrated to this country still maintain their own style of cooking, their manner of living, their own customs and language. This approach to life is sentimental. They are not adjusting to the food which is natural to the new place they are in: they are maintaining the same food customs of the old country. Many people are sentimentally attached to their old food customs. People sometimes long to have the same food they ate when they were children, and seek to recreate the style of cooking their mother used to do.

Romantic candlelight dinners are also on the emotional level. When you find a girlfriend or boyfriend, and you go to a restaurant, you do not necessarily go because the food is delicious. Rather, you go because you want to absorb the mood of that place—the decor, the music, the atmosphere. These are all examples of the sentimental way of eating.

4. Intellectual Eating This is the nutritional way of eating. This is the level of eating where there is much concern about the amount of calories you are taking in, the amount of vitamins you are taking in, the amount of protein you are taking in. The recommendations of dietitians and nutritionists are on this level. Large universities have departments of nutrition issuing guidelines on how much to eat, how much of each vitamin and mineral to take in each day. This is a big business. And yet most housewives do not measure calories, or proteins, or vitamins when they are shopping or cooking.

Analyzing food nutritionally is relatively new; it has only been used for the past fifty or sixty years. For thousands of years before that people were eating non-intellectually. So people are not used to approaching food consumption in this conceptual way. So far this method of eating is entirely impractical, and yet, in the modern world, it is considered to be the top level of eating.

So far, the levels of eating are more or less personal or individual in their approach. The second level of eating is making the food industry happy. The third one is making interior decorators happy. The fourth one is making colleges and universities happy. But as we approach the fifth level of eating, we begin to see a group consciousness appearing. This is the social way of eating.

5. Social Eating This is the level of eating where group consciousness begins. It is the level which regulates food distribution. This distribution can be dealt either fairly or unfairly, depending upon the moral conscience of the people involved. On this level, morality, fairness, ethics, and economic judgment take place.

For example, in the intellectual way of eating, doctors will advise that you eat animal protein every day. But when you see an overview of the population of the entire world, you see that only a small percentage of the population consumes animal protein on a regular basis. Most people cannot afford it. Yes, in the United States many people may be able to afford animal protein, but this population is small in comparison to the rest of the world. How many people can afford vitamin tablets? Even though vitamin C may be good, and many nutritionists are recommending that we drink orange juice every day, how many people in the world can afford that? Even though the nutritional theory says we need to take a certain amount of fat or oil every day, how many people can afford that?

It is on the fifth level of eating that these problems are confronted and decided. We determine what is social justice with regard to the food we are consuming. We determine what is the most economically justifiable method of eating. Instead of eating plenty of food every day, we begin to take the whole world population into account and consider the distribution of food throughout the world. We begin to eat less so that everybody in the world can have their fair share. And even though you can afford to eat plenty of food, still you eat in a humble way, and you give your surplus to other people. Although this is the beginning of social and planetary consciousness, it is not the highest level of eating.

6. Ideological Eating This is the way of eating according to a discipline or doctrine or a teaching. It may be a religious or spiritual teaching, or it may be one of the great teachings, such as the kosher laws established by Moses. Buddha also taught the way of eating. Macrobiotics is one of these great teachings. It is the way of longevity, the way of health. However, some people confuse the foods of macrobiotics with macrobiotics itself. They think that brown rice or azuki beans are "macrobiotic." But this view is incorrect. Brown rice is brown rice. Azuki beans are azuki beans. They are foods that we can use for macrobiotics, for the way of health, for the way of longevity. People often become confused by this.

When people eat on the ideological level they are inspired and guided by some form of doctrine or discipline. People who ate this way in the past did not concern themselves with the nutritional analysis of food; they did not worry about the vitamin content of the foods they were eating. They were more concerned with the discipline or principle of their doctrine. It may have been a principle of nature or a principle of life that they were recognizing. This was their main concern.

7. Supreme Eating This is free eating. Free eating is eating according to one's choice. It is eating according to one's dream. He or she simply eats. That is the highest way of eating. When you would like to see a certain dream, you design your food and you eat accordingly. Then you will start to see that dream. When you would like to see small things, such as a dream of your sweetheart, or perhaps some event, then you can eat in order to accomplish this end, and you will see it. In ancient times, it was easy for people to see whatever dream they wanted to see. But now, in the modern world, it has become increasingly difficult. However, when we know the importance of food and the way to achieve balance and harmony through daily eating, we can recover the ability to create our dreams.

Stages of Dream

Just as there are different levels of eating, there are different levels of dream. Our dreams develop in stages. The dreams we have as we grow from childhood to adulthood are more or less sensory and sentimental. Dreams of love affairs, struggles, falling from a high place, or being late for an appointment are on the sensory and emotional levels. As your consciousness develops, you begin to reason and think in a more intellectual way, and you may start to see dreams of invention, detection, problem solving, theorizing, and organizing.

The stories of Sherlock Holmes are nothing but the dreams of Sir Arthur Conan Doyle. They were on the intellectual level. In the same way, new discoveries are often made at night while you are sleeping. For example, a scientist may be intensely struggling with a certain equation. After many days of trying unsuccessfully to solve the problem, one night, the solution appears suddenly in a dream. Possibly you have had a similar experience. That kind of dream has nothing to do with suffering, sadness, or romance because the brain is working on a different level. Few people have dreams of this type, although everyone has the potential. Most dreams are sensory or sentimental.

On the next level, our dreams are more social. Gandhi, for example, had a social dream. His dream was to free India from British colonization. As a part of his dream, he went to England to study, and upon returning to India, participated in revolutionary activities. Gandhi and his associates were put in jail on numerous occasions and faced hunger and difficulties. Thousands of people died in the course of their struggle. Finally, after many years, they achieved their dream. Gandhi had carried the dream of Indian independence both day and night for much of his life.

Then, beyond the social level, your dream expands into the ideological realm. Here you try to solve basic questions such as, What is the order of the universe?, What is life?, What is happiness?, What is sickness?, What is health?, From where have we come? Day and night you struggle with these questions. Sometimes the answer will come in a true dream. Sometimes you see dreams in which the answer is not correct. Until a true dream appears, the solution does not come.

George Ohsawa had such a true dream while he was struggling to prove the theory of atomic transmutation (see *The*

Philosopher's Stone, One Peaceful World Press, 1994.) Although the concept of transmutation intrigued Ohsawa, he knew he lacked the technical expertise to conduct an actual experiment. So he sought the help of an old friend who was a brilliant chemist. They had become friends when Ohsawa was studying at the Sorbonne in the 1930s. After finishing his education, the friend had worked for a large chemical concern in France, and eventually became the head of research and development for that company. Ohsawa had lost touch with him during the war, but managed to locate him years later when he became interested by transmutation.

For several months, the two men grappled with the problem of how to change sodium into potassium in the laboratory without finding a solution. As a last resort, Ohsawa decided to go on diet number seven (a whole grain fast) until he discovered the answer.

I received a special delivery letter from Ohsawa a short time later. In it he stated that the answer had finally come to him in a dream. Since he had been eating well, he thought the dream must have been a true dream. Every day he was thinking about the experiment. One night he had a dream in which he saw a dark sky. A huge hand appeared above the earth. The hand made a motion as if it were catching something and throwing it down to earth. Each time the hand closed, thunder, lightning, and sparks arose. Then, on the surface of the earth, some type of shiny metal was created when the sparks collided with the ground.

When Ohsawa woke up, he understood that an electric arc would be necessary for the experiment. Guided by the image in the dream, he utilized a small, simple vacuum tube. To generate the electric arc, he placed two electrodes, one positive and the other negative, at either end of the tube. He placed sodium in the vacuum tube, activated the electrodes, and then introduced oxygen. The sodium fused with the oxygen to form potassium. The experiment was a success, and led to a variety of other experiments that proved that atomic transmutation could be performed at low temperature, low pressure, and low energy.

In a similar way, before I give a lecture, I do not take

several hours to prepare. I prepare quickly because of a busy schedule, usually taking only fifteen minutes to a half-an-hour. During that time, I keep myself quiet and try to formulate a true dream or image. Then I know how to proceed.

Dreams can tell you many things. The important thing is whether we are seeing a true dream or an illusory dream. If we are always nourishing our bodies with good food and we want to discover something, definitely the answer will come either during the day or at night in the form of a dream. That is the amazing thing everyone can discover for himself. There is no need to depend on others. Just keep eating well and really try to find out the solution.

The last form of dream is the dream of infinity, eternity, and absoluteness. This dream never changes. It was the same a thousand years ago, and will be the same a thousand years from now. It is universal and permanent. When you start to see that dream, then you discover true happiness. No matter who you are, where you are, or what you are doing, you see a dream that never changes and never ends. All the other levels of dream eventually disappear, but an infinite dream continues forever.

Our smaller dreams are nothing but tools to realize our biggest dream. They are not our real purpose. If the tools do not work, we must change them, especially if they do not work for everyone's health and happiness.

We need to see a universal, permanent dream and eliminate our illusory dreams. You can see that dream day and night, and devote your whole life to realizing it. To seek means to grow. A baby starts to crawl, then stands, walks, and starts to talk. The baby is always seeking. In the same way, we must continually seek and continually grow. Not physically, but mentally and spiritually. Then, at the age of twenty, fifty, or ninety, you see the same dream and pursue the same goal. Of course, the means or method may change, but the same spirit is there—even after you die, because this dream never ends. Eternally we are pursuing this endless dream. That is happiness. Without dream there is no life. Our life is equal to our dream.

7
The Reality of Dreams

There are two kinds of dreams. There is the dream you have at night, which is nothing more than images projected on your mind. But there is also the kind of dream which you have during the day. Your life is nothing more than a dream. In addition, there are many people, especially in the primitive areas of Africa and the South Pacific, who believe that dreams are not separate from daily life. When they have a dream, they really believe that they have actually experienced it. For example, if a boy dreams that he has married a girl from the next village, then he goes to that village and speaks to that girl's father. He is then given the girl for his wife.

Whatever they dream they treat as reality. Everyone throughout the world was doing this, until the so-called "civilized" world began. So for them there was no difference between day and night. There was no difference between dream and reality. What they think is reality.

What kind of reality do you wish to create? You can do it when you reach the seventh level of eating. That seventh level was practiced all over the world by many people. They were creating their own reality. So, if you would like to see the dream of war, or if you would like to bring war into the world, eat meat every day. Then you can materialize your dream. If you would like to be a great musician, then you have to eat strong yang and strong yin, especially fruits. The yang will give you the strength to play your instrument, and the yin will give you the sensitivity to make nice music. The yang could be meat or it could be fish. Bach, for instance, did not eat much meat, but he did eat whole grain bread, and a lot of salt. If you like to paint portraits, if you would like to be a successful businessman, if you would like to be a great teacher, if you would like to be a powerful warrior, you can design your way of eating accordingly. You can make up your own menu according to what your dream is. If you eat a certain way, then you change into what you want. You will see life according to that way, and you will be able to act in that manner. That is the seventh level of eating. That way of eating is what we call *real* macrobiotic eating. That is the free person's way of eating.

Now you know how to orient and produce your life dream. Many people still do not understand the cause of their thinking which produces their dreams and images. So, when they have a dream, they want to interpret it. But, before the image comes, we had better create that image in the manner we wish it to be. If you can do that, you can create your image and your life dream.

Life Dream

There are seven levels of life dream. You can become rich; you can enjoy life, you can have many mistresses (that is on the second level); you can invent or discover something (that is on the fourth level); you can be a great spiritual leader like Moses (that is on the sixth level); you can be a person of justice, a person of fairness (that is on the fifth level). There are many levels upon which you can form your dream. The level upon which you form your dream is determined largely by your physical and mental constitution and health.

If you are blind you do not think about using your eyes. You do not think about becoming a great painter. Rather, you would think about becoming a great thinker, which you can be without using your eyes. If you cannot hear, then you do not choose to become a great musician. Rather, you choose to become a great scholar, which you can do without using your ears. In the same respect, you choose your life dream according to what level of judgment you are on. You do not think about becoming something on a different level, because it would be inappropriate for you. You orient your life for the realization of your dream, and you produce it. No one can do anything in opposition to his constitution. Everyone, without any assistance, is doing exactly what he wants to do, by the choice of his or her physical condition.

Some people want to become farmers, to go back to the land. Other people do not want to do that. And yet they know that farming is fine, it is just that they do not want to live in the country. They would rather live in the town. Their condition is different, physically different. No one can say that if you do not like the country you are bad. We cannot say that. If you wish to stay in the city, it is because your constitution prefers it.

The orientation of your dream is determined by your physical constitution. And this constitution is created for the most part by your mother. The father contributes to a certain extent. But it is the mother who is largely responsible for the constitution of her children. Her way of eating, her way of thinking determines for the most part the constitution of her children. In this way the kind of dream a person has is decided at an early age. The constitution of the person which determines the life dream is given to the child in the womb. That is why so many great persons have had strong mothers. The strength of the mother is vitally important in determining the direction of the child's life dream.

Some people have a small dream. Other people have a large dream. The bigger the life dream, the better. If you have a small dream, that means you are a small person. If your dream is big, that means you are a big person. The method of determining whether you have a small dream or a large dream is not dependent upon how much money you have. You may not have much money at all. The person who has a billion dollars may have a much smaller dream than you. The scale of your dream is not one of monetary value. The same thing applies to social position and fame. Neither of these things apply to the scale of your dream. You may not have any friends now, you may not have a wife or a husband, but when you are thinking of your life dream in the perspective of the entire universe, these things matter little.

What determines the scale of different dreams? When you see the dream, why do some people see it in a small way, while others see it in a large way? The midbrain needs to be yang in order to see the dream in a big way. Yangness is the state of vacuum, or emptiness. In that case, the inside becomes more compacted while the outside becomes more relaxed. The hara is centered and yang, while the periphery is relaxed. This kind of person is strong on the inside, yet yielding on the surface. On the surface this kind of person is kind, generous, and affectionate. But inside this person knows what he wants and how to achieve it. He has "backbone." He does not need to surrender under any condition. This is the ideal type of character.

The Beginning of Dream

The life dream is your dream, so it cannot be told to you by someone else. Yes, you can seek advice and encouragement from other people. But your dream can only be decided by you. It is your life to live. And only you can set its direction. You do not need to depend upon anyone—your parents, your peer group, your guru, books, great teachings, anything. You yourself need to choose your life dream.

In order to do that it is important to be like a child; almost naive, with an empty mind. Children regard the universe with great admiration. In that way, you can always be genuinely yourself. You need not think that you must enter into someone else's college or doctrine or way in order to fulfill your dream. Choose your dream by yourself. Make yourself a simple person. And from that mental state you can see the whole world, the whole universe. Then your own dream can develop.

So many people are living other people's dreams. Thus they are frustrated. When they die at the age of sixty-five, seventy, or seventy-five, they are so sorry that they did not do what they really wanted to do. They spent their entire lives working for some company or corporation or movement or whatever, and they did not do, they did not know what they really wanted to do. But when everyone was born, they had the innate ability to choose what they wanted to do in life. This ability is often clouded by school education. It is hidden. What was once a clear dream becomes covered up with social responsibility. Our original dream becomes coated, colored by those "disciplines." And we forgot what our dream really was. Therefore, we must resurrect our native judgment in order to see our own unique dream. Then we will know what it is that we would like to do while we are here on this earth. That is the starting point to forming our life dream.

Direction of the Dream

In order to set the direction of the life dream we must have a compass which even in the darkness can point out our direction. We need a compass which, even in the bright daylight with its distraction of people and television and ideas and thoughts, can safely guide us through. We need a compass to constantly keep us going in the direction we really want to go in.

We can build a compass in two ways:

1. We can build the compass internally. We can build it up through our bodies.
2. We can build the compass mentally. We can build it up through our changing mentality.

In these two ways you can build up your compass. You can use either method. If you can use both, it is very good.

In order to build the compass internally, we need to change the quality of our hemoglobin. That is the most direct method. Since the core of hemoglobin is iron, the best way to change the iron core of our red blood cells is to eat vegetable quality food. The core of chlorophyll is magnesium. In the body, magnesium fuses with oxygen and, through a process of transmutation, changes into iron. Unlike the iron found in meat and other animal foods, the iron produced by transmutation does not rust. It is important that we create the highest quality iron in our blood because iron is magnetic and reacts to the magnetic North Pole. Thus it helps us maintain our direction.

The quality of people's internal compass has become weak in modern times. Many people's compasses do not point toward the direction they want to go in. Rather it has become wishy-washy. That is the beginning of confusion. People are often presented with too many directions to go in. The iron from some hemoglobin points this way. The iron in other hemoglobin points that way. That is confusion. Maybe this is right. Maybe that is right. I don't know. I cannot choose.

In order to avoid such confusion, we need to build up our internal compass. The iron in our red blood cells comes from our food. So the internal compass is built up directly from the food we eat. Now suppose we take drugs or use a lot of medication. If we receive a wound, the normal reaction of the white blood cells is to rush to the opening and protect it from the invasion of bacteria. But with the introduction of drugs into the bloodstream, the white blood cells become confused and are unable to go directly to the wound. They get sidetracked and distracted. They just float around. They have lost their direction.

The same thing happens when we take sugar. The white blood cells become wishy-washy. A similar reaction happens to the red blood cells when we are suffering from anemia. This phenomenon occurs when there is a larger proportion of white blood cells to red blood cells. At that time the red blood cells cannot flow in a straight line, they move in an erratic course. That directly influences our judgment.

Red blood cells are yang; white blood cells are yin. We need to maintain good balance between the yin and yang elements. This applies to the yin and yang of our blood cells. Healthy red blood cells are yang. If you see the color of healthy blood, it is a rich red. It is not a dirty red color—like a black-red or brown, sometimes toward greenish. This is not healthy. Nor is healthy blood thin and pale in color. Yes, everyone has a different shade of red to their blood, but ideally, this color should be a rich, true red. If the color of your blood is healthy, then the iron core of your hemoglobin is sensitive to the attraction of magnetism. You do not have just one piece of iron in your bloodstream, you have trillions of tiny particles of magnetic iron, all pointing to the North Pole. Thus we have an internal compass working for us.

In order to build up our thinking compass, we must orient our abstract thinking. To do this it is important to think in terms of yin and yang. In this way we can develop our judgment. For example, in a certain circumstance we are becoming sad and miserable. We have many difficulties. If at that time we think according to yin and yang, we can realize that we are in a yin aspect of our life and that soon it will pass. Soon we will be in a happy, more yang aspect. If we think in this way, we can develop the patience to pass through the more depressing moments in life. We can let the experience of the sadness or depression pass right through us. But the opposite is also true. When we experience good fortune, when things go well for us, we must remember that the bigger the front, the bigger the back. If we indulge heavily in our good fortune, then perhaps misfortune will soon follow. If we are healthy and happy right now, we must be prepared for possible unhappiness. What we must be most wary of is pride. It is better not to be boastful. All too easily, health and happiness can change into misfortune.

If we think according to yin and yang, we can understand the ephemerality of both good fortune and misfortune.

It is ideal if you have both the internal compass and the thinking compass working for you. But if you have the internal compass, without the understanding of yin and yang, it will be all right. In the same respect, if you have only the thinking compass of yin and yang, then you can likewise orient your life positively. These two compasses are the front and back of each other. It is much better to have them both. That way you will avoid confusion. But it is possible to go with just one of them. The internal compass alone can make you happy, but not entirely. The thinking compass alone becomes conceptual, and cannot help you realize step-by-step, day-by-day, the path to the fulfillment of your dream. But the uniqueness of the macrobiotic principle is that even a sick person can go by means of the thinking compass. And this can be helpful to them.

Scale of the Dream

The scale of your dream depends upon you yourself. However large you wish your dream to be, it will be.

The scale of your dream is determined by the size of your appetite. If you have a large appetite, you will likely have a large dream. If you have a small appetite, you will likely have a small dream.

In order to have a big appetite, we need to make ourselves hungry. Hunger brings about a big appetite. In addition to that, it is better to surround yourself with challenges. The combination of hunger and challenges helps us to develop our appetite so that we can have a large dream. If you eat too much, if you are living comfortably, you have no space in which to create a dream. You just lie down on the sofa and watch television. You sleep your way through life. If you are hungry, then you will get up and seek food. The same thing happens with your life. If you are comfortable, then you are content with your satisfaction. But if you are not fulfilled, then you will seek to satisfy this hunger.

You can now understand that the family life of most great people had to be simple. They had to experience hunger and difficulties in order to create their dream. Their parents and grandparents were living a simple life. And often in childhood, these persons had to experience many skipped meals. This hunger and difficulties and simple life strengthened their constitutions, but also gave them a foundation from which to create their dream.

Generally, the bigger the hunger, the bigger the dream. This is perhaps the most important factor in the development of the life dream—hunger and difficulties. This is what George Ohsawa called "adventure." If you are living now in comfortable circumstances, then create difficulties for yourself. Then you can challenge these difficulties and your dream can grow. Do not stay in comfortable surroundings; you will wither away. The worst thing in life is not becoming sick, not losing your money, not divorcing your wife or husband. The worst thing is to lose your life dream. To lose your dream is to be dead while you are still living. You have nothing to live for. Nothing to do. If you see yourself losing your dream, or if your dream is becoming small, then shake yourself up. Make more difficulties for yourself. Put yourself in more challenging circumstances. Then you can recreate your dream. You can bring yourself back to life.

There are so many challenges in life. Once you know how to help others heal themselves, can you be satisfied to leave so many sick people alone? Wouldn't you like to help them? If you want to help one person, your life will continue. That kind of challenge will keep you alive.

Quality of the Dream

There are many kinds of dream. Thomas Jefferson had a dream in which he envisioned a nation dedicated to individual freedom. He chose that dream. And he selected means by which he felt he could achieve his dream. He felt he could bring about a better society. Tolstoy wrote many books because he felt that was the way to bring about a better society.

There are many ways to create and implement a dream. Even though you have a dream, the manner in which you enact your dream forms the content or quality of that dream.

What determines the quality of your dream? Some people have a violent quality to their dream. Some people have a noisy manner. Some people prefer a quiet, solitary way. Some people mobilize masses of people. Some stay in the forest, like Thoreau.

On a practical level, what determines the quality of our dream is the quality of the food we eat. The food consumed from childhood determines the quality of the dream. If we have eaten a lot of animal food, we would tend more toward warfare and violence. If we have eaten a lot of fruit, we would tend toward a more gentle or artistic way.

There are several factors that go into making the life dream. The most important one is the food we eat. The next most important factor is the social conditions in which we live—whether we have difficulties or not. The third is the quality of our thinking.

Simply speaking, to form a big dream, it is necessary to have a good, strong, healthy mother. In addition, put yourself in challenging surroundings. Difficulties help you develop, as does a simple environment. With this kind of background you can have a good foundation for forming and actualizing your dream. In addition to a good foundation, you need to feed your dream every day and keep it growing. In order to do this, eat good food every day. Think and study every day. Test life situations and circumstances with the principle of yin and yang. It is also important to be physically active, and to have many experiences. The food of thinking is yin food. The food of activity is yang food. Together they form a balanced diet.

Endless Dream

Ideally, there should be no limit to your dream. Your dream can become really big, even infinite. Your body, your life has a limit. It has a beginning and an end. Everyone will die someday. Yet it is strange that your dream is endless. Why is it that although we are limited in our physical existence, our dream can be endless? Why is it that our dream can go from generation to generation, even ten generations, a thousand generations?

You formed your dream long before you took on this physical form. You willed to be born. Your created your own body. Now that we have this body, we create images that are dreams which we can realize. So, before we were born the image of our dream was there. And after we die, still our dream will be there. This body we are living in is nothing but a materialized toy with which we are playing. We created it with our dream. We materialized it so that we could play on this earth. Thus it is ephemeral. But our dream is eternal. So we can say that our human life is nothing but a dream.

Do not be content with a small dream. Small dreams receive only a tiny fraction of the vibrations coming from the infinite universe. A person with a small dream is thinking only of himself or his family. A person with a large dream is thinking of society, of the whole world. The amount of vibrations from the infinite universe that can be picked up by us depends upon our receiver. When it is hungry and wanting, then it will receive many vibrations. If we are full, then we cannot pick up any vibrations even from a short distance.

Originally we shared the same dream, but because of the quality of our receiver, the interpretation of that dream is different for each person. Someone who is thin has a sharper receiver than someone who is overweight. If the eyes are far apart, our vision will be scattered. If they are close together, our vision becomes too narrow. If the eyes are set in a balanced place on our face, we can develop a big dream. We should be able to reach our whole body with our hands. If we cannot, then we are too rigid—our receiver will be too tight to receive a wide range of vibrations. Since each person has a different physical condition, there are varied interpretations of the shared dream.

Man is the son of dream. Woman, however, is the creator of the dream. Women create through their ability to cook, and by their way of eating. A woman creates children, and creates her husband or sweetheart. She helps them realize their dream. When a woman chooses a husband or partner, she is attracted to someone who has a wonderful dream. She wants to feed that dream, to nourish and make it perfect. So, sometimes we are the actor of our dream, and sometimes we are the director. The important thing to remember is that we should have a big dream. We should remain healthy so that we can realize our dream. We should maintain a good receiver so that we can receive the vibrations from the infinite universe. We should always maintain a good appetite so that we can keep our dream big, and help it to grow again if it begins to fade. Have a big dream. You will become big.

8
Universal Dream

"As there is no screen or ceiling between our heads and the infinite heavens, so is there no bar or wall in the soul, where man, the effect, ceases, and God, the cause, begins."—Emerson

Our body is a reflection of our environment, of the spiritual and physical food that we daily consume and transmute into ourselves. The vegetable kingdom provides the material from which our physical bodies are made. In human beings, vegetable quality changes into animal quality and is the origin of our animal body. The vegetable kingdom has come from the earth, water, sun, and air, or, in other words, the world of nature.

Over a hundred elements make up the natural world. The vegetable kingdom contains thousands of species, and there are millions of species within the animal world. Elements arise from preatomic particles, such as electrons and protons. Here there are about thirty-two classifications. Beyond the world of preatomic particles is the world of vibration, or waves. In this realm there are about eight distinct classifications. This world of vibrations comes from the world of two poles, the primary origin of differentiation. We may call this the world of polarization, or yin and yang, as ancient Oriental people did, or use other terms. Polarization is preceded by oneness or infinity.

We materialized along these seven stages in the motion of a contracting, centripetal spiral. From the seventh world of infinity, we came to the present world as a human being. There is no separation between these worlds. Each stage of the spiral is based on, and is inseparable from, all those that have preceded it. The seventh heaven, or infinity, is always present, not past, not future, not separated from us, but always here, now. Thus, infinity is the source of our endless, eternal dream.

The sixth world, or the world of yin and yang, is the beginning of the phenomenal, relative world that we experience day to day. We perceive part of this phenomenal world with our senses and our feelings, as well as through our relative, changing dreams. The world of yin and yang, however, is hidden from our senses and our experiences, and the infinite cannot be differentiated at all.

In the relative world, we can experience distinctions of time and space, both through our day-to-day consciousness, and in our dreams. But the infinite world is not relative. That means that even a billion light years distance can be reached instantaneously, since infinity has no space and no time. Thus, time-wise, there is only the present, and space-wise, there is only the here. You may say that the here and now is the same as the infinite world. During sleep, we perceive the infinite world as the state of no dreams; the state of pure non-consciousness.

In the infinite world, what we did yesterday or what we will do tomorrow, is always experienced in the present. But as we go toward the relative world of human experience, there is a greater sense of past and future, and of separation. The relative world is the source of relative, changing dreams, including the illusory dreams that arise from excess in our diet.

Why and how have we come to this world from the world of infinite dream. Infinity did not "create" us, but changed itself, within itself, and manifested in various forms, including humanity. We are manifestations of the infinite universe, just as is everything in nature. All things, everywhere, are nothing but changing forms of the infinite, and are nothing but different representations of infinite dream.

We cannot separate ourselves from the world of infinite

dream. No phenomena can be isolated from infinity. Whatever we do, whatever we think, whatever we dream, before we were born and after we die, we, and all things, are manifestations of the infinite one. If we believe we are separate from the infinite, we are revealing our delusion based upon the limited perception of the senses.

Seeing a differentiated universe, instead of a total view, we perceive the human population of about five billion as separated beings. Each of these five billion, respectively, thinks that he or she is the center. As a result, they see only the relative world and relative dreams. These five billion manifestations are all within one world, within one universe, within one infinity. Therefore, our origin is the same, the way in which we have manifested ourselves is the same, and the law of change that governs our destiny, as well as the destiny of everything else, is also the same. Our future direction, as well as our past, is the same. Our original country, the infinite, which is also our future, is the same. Therefore, our endless dream is also the same. Infinity is not manifested within us, nor without us, but as us. We are the manifestations of one infinite universe.

Although we share a common origin, destiny, and dream with all humanity, our individual quality, development, and dream depend on our understanding of the order of the universe. People live from various levels of consciousness and thus experience different dreams. The difference between people is determined by how well they understand the order of the universe. When we see only from the eyes of our human body, we develop a theoretical or analytical view. By making ourselves the center we analyze and evaluate different phenomena, and our world and our dreams become more and more fragmented. By this way of seeing we have created our modern-day civilization. A totally opposite way to view life is from the viewpoint of infinity. When we have an object, for instance, a piece of paper, we know that infinity comes into both sides. If we bend this into an almost closed circle, we tend to become confused. We can still understand that the outside influences are coming from infinity, but we forget that the inside influences do also. There is nothing which does not have an entrance and an exit.

Our infinite environment is always creating us; is continuously coming in and going out. Our big entrance is our mouth, and our big exit is our digestive tract and our skin through which we discharge sweat and heat radiation. This constant entering and exiting we call the stream of the outer world. Our body is small and dense, its motion is rapid. The radiation which we continuously discharge is called our personality or spirituality, and also our thoughts and dreams. Therefore, the composition of our body, as well as the quality of our dreams, did not originate from the inside. It came from the outside.

Constantly, day after day, the external environment enters our bodies in the form of spiritual and physical vibrations. From these vibrations, various spirals create our different organs and body parts, which in turn are constantly discharging vibration toward the outside, including in the form of dreams. Therefore, nothing within us ever stays still. All is constantly changing. Vibrations enter from the outside, and form our organs and bodily systems, and are continually begin discharged toward the outside. What we take in from the outside and how we discharge it, controls our bodies and our destiny.

Our inner and outer worlds are both infinity; their origin is the same. Our body and the entire environment, or you may say, the world of nature, are not two; they are one. Our body is the manifestation of nature, the universe, or God. So the order which governs our body, nature, and the invisible world of dreams is one. The law and mechanism are the same.

Seeing an Infinite Dream

To be healthy and happy in this life, we need to live in a way that is harmonious with the law of nature, or you may say, yin and yang. To develop an endless, infinite dream, we need to see ourselves from the eyes of the universe, and not only from the eyes of the body.

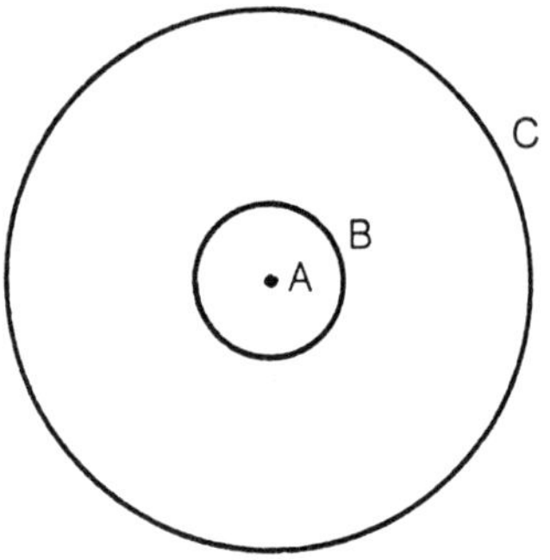

The diagram above gives three different views of earth: A, B, and C. Our life on earth is an infinitesimal reflection of life. Let us try to see ourselves and the earth from the outside. If we move away from the planet, it becomes smaller, and if we continue further, it becomes a point in space that eventually vanishes. From this perspective, our human life also disappears. This view is something like the view of God, the infinite universe, in which we understand how ephemeral life is. Even if we conquer the whole world, or build a great civilization or empire, it must eventually disappear like the morning dew. Whatever good or bad things we do in this life will vanish. When we know the ephemerality of life, we are beginning to see with the eyes of the universe and can begin to see an endless dream.

The thought that we live for a long time is only an illusion. When we say we are living infinitely, or that our dream is eternal, what we mean is that we are living as the infinite universe, not as a human being. Our life is eternal, our dream is eternal, and we change eternally. This is the world of infinity, not the world of human beings. The following practice can help you develop this vision.

First, look at the above diagram. Concentrate on world

"C" and hold that image for a while, imagining that you are living on the surface of the earth with billions of other people. Then, imagine that you are going further away and see the earth as "B." Keep your concentration there for about one minute. Then go further away until the earth is as small as point "A." Concentrate on that for about one minute, and then, in your imagination, go further away until you see the earth disappear in the darkness of space. Now you are in the realm of infinite dream.

To return to the relative world, begin with an image of the darkness of space and slowly start to see the earth as a small speck. Come closer and closer toward the earth, seeing it become ever larger as you do so. This is mediation in which a universal dream becomes increasingly relative and changeable. Please continue to do these two meditations so as to develop your ability to see an endless, eternal dream and to evaluate your personal dreams from a universal perspective. Learn to see yourself from heaven and know the reality—and the ephemerality—of your life.

The Source of Dreams

Of the seven stages on the spiral of materialization, which determines your destiny, your life direction, your will? Also, which level creates desire, such as wanting to eat when hungry, or wanting possessions when we are poor? Similarly, which level produces true dreams, and from which level do illusory dreams arise?

Desires arise from level number one, or our human body. This is also the origin of various illusory dreams. When we decided to be born as a human being on the earth, was that a result of desire or will? It was a result of will. When we grow from a baby to an adult, is that because of will or desire? Even though we may not want to, in any case we grow. This is our inevitable course, or will. This will determines the direction of life, or our destiny. We may not want to die, and may want to live forever, but this is only our desire.

Suppose we want to go to a restaurant and eat ice cream.

Is this our will or desire? This results from our desire, which is not our overall direction, but only a result of relative relationships. Our will is the overall course from infinity or God to the relative, infinitesimal world and back again to infinity. Through the natural process of will, we experience frequent births and deaths through all seven levels of the spiral. We may consider will to be the huge current or stream of life active at all these levels. True dreams are the product of this huge current of universal will, and are not the product of our individual desires.

We are always going in the same direction as will, and are inevitably being carried along by this stream of life. Our will does not mean the desires of our "small I." These are nothing but waves upon the large stream of life, or will. Waves may go up and down, or if an obstacle is in the way, they may be deflected backward. These waves are like the desires of our small I, which are a part of manifestation of will. Similarly, dreams come and go, appear and disappear. They are the individual manifestation of true dream.

Will is our universal, infinite self. We cannot avoid our ultimate destiny, because that is our will, which is the same as the will of the universe, or the current of life. Everyone is going along with this regardless of their desires. Desires and individual or illusory dreams are fluctuations within the endless stream of life. When we chose our parents, was it because of will or desire? Will. When we decided to be born on the earth, was it will or desire? Will.

Does our dream, our ideal, or our vision of the future form our will or our desire? We have two basic kinds of dreams. Nightmares and illusory dreams arise from the world of desire. But, when you have a dream that you would like to be perfect, to create peace, or to become a fully-loving person, in harmony with everyone, this is the same as will. Why do we form a dream of peace, harmony, and love? Which world is the world of peace, harmony, and love? Number seven. We all know that the world of man and the world of God are not the same. Our everyday experience does not include only peace, harmony, and love. Yet we all have a dream of becoming the same as the world of God.

If we did not know the world of God, we would not have such a dream, which means that we have memory. Why do we have memory of perfect peace, harmony, and love? Because we once were infinity, or God itself. We have now manifested ourselves into this world, but still carry the image or memory of the absolute world, and so we wish to move in that direction. So, our dream equals our memory. Since our memory is there, we can dream.

We were once in this state of absolute freedom, happiness, and peace but are now in the most ephemeral world, the world of ceaseless change. Just as everyone is born, grows, and eventually dies, so everyone has the dream of freedom, love, and peace, and wants to seek and realize it. We all want to experience heaven on earth. Through our human life we fulfill this dream, both within our own lives and in society. This is the way of our real self. Wanting to eat ice cream or win the lottery is only our small desire, not the infinite current of will.

If we see with the eyes of the universe, we realize that we chose our parents, we were born upon this earth, we grew, and we are going to die. Or, as Shakespeare put it: "Thou know'st 'tis common; all that lives must die, passing through nature to eternity." That is our destiny, or real direction dictated by our will. This means that even though we are living in the world of man, we do not forget the world of God. Even though we are an ephemeral, physical manifestation on this earth, we are always living with our real selves, never forgetting our origin. In everyday life, this means that we should always see ourselves from the eyes of the universe, and never forget that we have come from infinity. This is our true freedom and happiness, and if we live in this way, we are living as God in this tiny realm.

We have forgotten from where we came. We assume that we are a product of heredity, that our mother and father created us. Many people think, "I did not intend to come here, and since this world is a terrible place, I will do whatever I want." This is living with desire, with relative illusory dreams. It is not a reflection of our infinite dream, but rather of limited, relative desire.

When we think that we would like to have this or that, or become this or that, we are living with our ephemeral dream based on desire. The more we have and the more we become, the more we emphasize this relative world and, as a result, the more unhappy we become. If this is what we want, we had better live quietly and alone, secluded from this ever-changing world. As we accentuate the world of desire, we forget our will, and how we came into this life, and that we have infinite life, and infinite dream. This creates endless problems. To be happy we must live always with this stream of will, dream, and memory.

We should view our life from the perspective of the infinite universe, which means that we must not forget from where we came and to where we are going. This also means that we should always try to realize our endless dream. In the human world this means a dream of happiness, health, and love. If, in our day to day lives, we try to realize this, our spiritual life as a human being has begun.

This endless dream existed before we became human beings, and it will continue after our death as our offspring carry it on. But, if our dream is based on ephemeral desires, then our children's dream will differ from ours. For example, suppose we want to become a businessman, our children may want to become politicians, and our grandchildren may choose to become gangsters. All desires are different. But, if our dream is a true dream, then our children, grandchildren, and future generations will be able to share it. This is because our dream and that of our children, and all of our offspring, generation after generation, are going in the same direction. Furthermore, this dream continues for us even after we are born into the next life. Then, when you are born into another world, your dream continues. We call this living our endless dream.

Resources

One Peaceful World is an international information network and friendship society devoted to the realization of one healthy, peaceful world. Activities include educational and spiritual tours, assemblies and forums, international food aid and development, and publishing. Membership is $30/year for individuals and $50 for families and includes a subscription to the *One Peaceful World Newsletter* and a free book from One Peaceful World Press. For further information, contact:

One Peaceful World
Box 10, Becket, MA 01223
(413) 623–2322
Fax (413) 623–8827

The Kushi Institute offers ongoing classes and seminars including those presented by Michio Kushi. For information, contact:

Kushi Institute
Box 7, Becket MA 01223
(413) 623–5741
Fax (413) 623–8827

Recommended Reading

1. Esko, Edward. *Basics and Benefits of Macrobiotics* (One Peaceful World Press, 1995).

2. Esko, Edward. *Notes from the Boundless Frontier* (One Peaceful World Press, 1992).

3. Esko, Edward. *The Pulse of Life* (One Peaceful World Press, 1994).

4. Esko, Wendy. *Rice Is Nice* (One Peaceful World Press, 1995).

5. Jack, Alex. *Profiles in Oriental Diagnosis* (One Peaceful World Press, 1995).

6. Kushi, Michio. *Basic Shiatsu* (with Edward Esko, One Peaceful World Press, 1995).

7. Kushi, Michio. *Forgotten Worlds* (with Edward Esko, One Peaceful World Press, 1992).

8. Kushi, Michio. *Healing Harvest* (with Edward Esko, One Peaceful World Press, 1994).

9. Kushi, Michio. *Holistic Health Through Macrobiotics* (with Edward Esko, Japan Publications, 1993).

10. Kushi, Michio. *Nine Star Ki* (with Edward Esko, One Peaceful World Press, 1991).

11. Kushi, Michio. *The Philosopher's Stone* (with Edward Esko, One Peaceful World Press, 1994).

12. Kushi, Michio. *Spiritual Journey* (with Edward Esko, One Peaceful World Press, 1994).

For a free catalog of macrobiotic books available by mail order, please write One Peaceful World Press, Box 10, Becket, MA 01223 or telephone (413) 623-2322.

About the Authors

Michio Kushi is the leader of the international macrobiotic community. Recipient of the United Nations' highest literary award, he lectures and advises governments and health organizations around the world. He is the author of many books including *The Cancer-Prevention Diet, Diet for a Strong Heart, One Peaceful World, Standard Macrobiotic Diet, The Gospel of Peace,* and *Basic Home Remedies.* He lives with his wife, Aveline, in Brookline, Massachusetts.

Edward Esko teaches healthcare and planetary ecology at the Kushi Institute and lectures in North America, Europe, the Far East, and around the world. He is the co-author, with Michio Kushi, of *Holistic Health through Macrobiotics, Nine Star Ki, Basic Shiatsu, Spiritual Journey, Healing Harvest,* and other books. He is co-founder of One Peaceful World Press, the leading publisher of macrobiotic books today, and author of *Basics and Benefits of Macrobiotics, Notes from the Boundless Frontier,* and *The Pulse of Life.* He lives with his wife, Wendy, a cooking teacher, and family in Becket, Mass.

Index

General Index

Index of Dream Symbols